HE PHILLIP KEVEREN SERIES

JAZZY TUNES

— PIANO LEVEL —
ELEMENTARY
(HLSPL LEVEL 2-3)

ISBN-13: 978-1-4234-2551-9
ISBN-10: 1-4234-2551-0

Hal•Leonard®
CORPORATION
7777 W. BLUEMOUND RD. P.O. BOX 13819 MILWAUKEE, WI 53213

Visit Hal Leonard Online at
www.halleonard.com
Visit Phillip at
www.phillipkeveren.com

PREFACE

This collection is chock full of pieces that feature catchy syncopations. Although these arrangements simplify the most difficult rhythms found in the original compositions, every effort was made to maintain the spirit that makes each song unique.

Listening to recordings will help you interpret these arrangements. You will broaden your understanding of the piece and expand your sense of musical style.

Have fun with these jazzy gems!

Sincerely,
Phillip Keveren

BIOGRAPHY

Phillip Keveren, a multi-talented keyboard artist and composer, has composed original works in a variety of genres from piano solo to symphonic orchestra. Mr. Keveren gives frequent concerts and workshops for teachers and their students in the United States, Canada, Europe, and Asia. Mr. Keveren holds a B.M. in composition from California State University Northridge and a M.M. in composition from the University of Southern California.

CONTENTS

4   **BABY ELEPHANT WALK**

10   **BEYOND THE SEA**

12   **BYE BYE BLACKBIRD**

14   **IN THE MOOD**

7   **IT DON'T MEAN A THING
(IF IT AIN'T GOT THAT SWING)**

16   **JEANNIE**

18   **LINUS AND LUCY**

22   **MAIRZY DOATS**

24   **NIGHT TRAIN**

26   **THE ODD COUPLE**

28   **OPUS ONE**

30   **SALT PEANUTS**

32   **SESAME STREET THEME**

34   **SUNNY**

36   **THE SURREY WITH THE FRINGE ON TOP**

38   **TUXEDO JUNCTION**

BABY ELEPHANT WALK
from the Paramount Picture HATARI!

By HENRY MANCINI
Arranged by Phillip Keveren

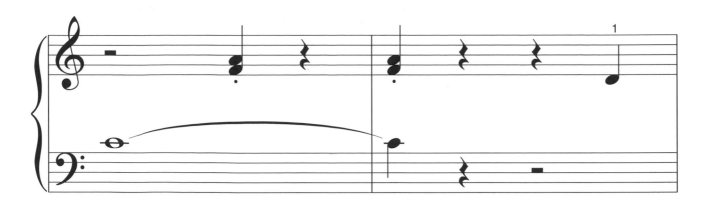

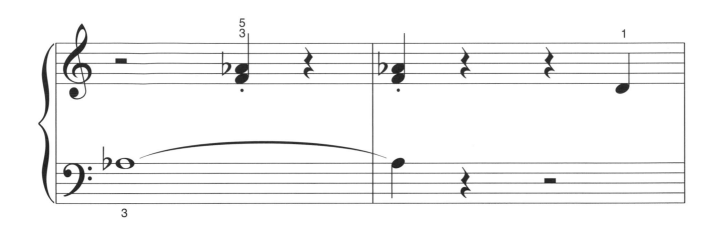

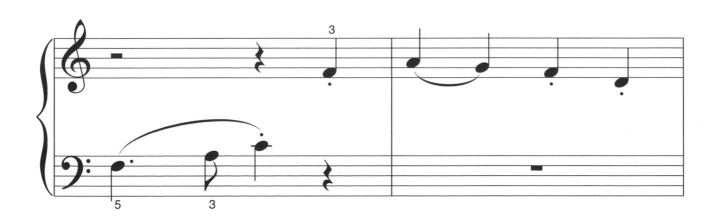

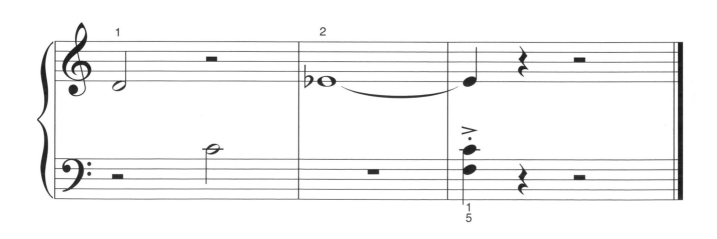

IT DON'T MEAN A THING
(If It Ain't Got That Swing)
from SOPHISTICATED LADIES

Words and Music by DUKE ELLINGTON
and IRVING MILLS
Arranged by Phillip Keveren

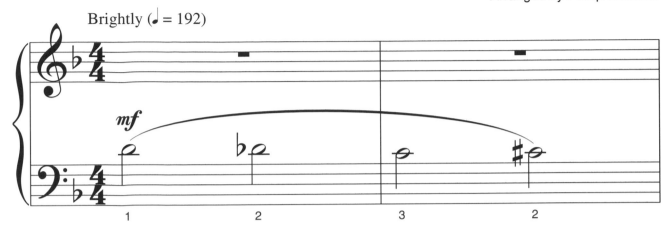

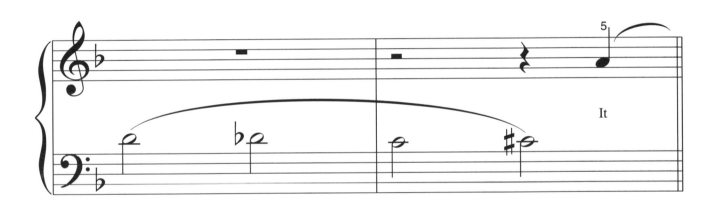

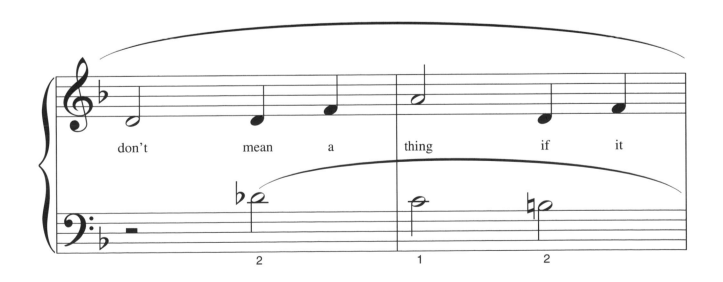

ain't   got   that   swing.

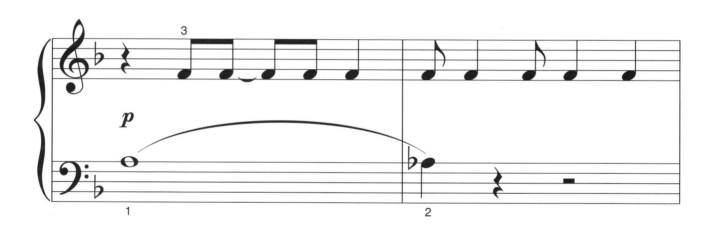

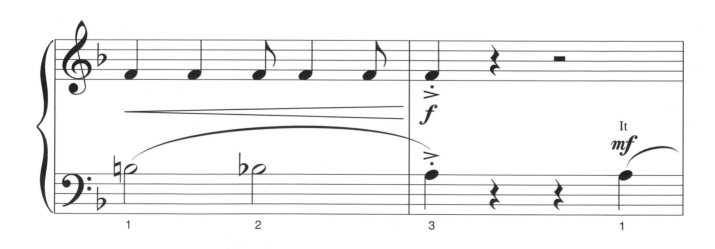

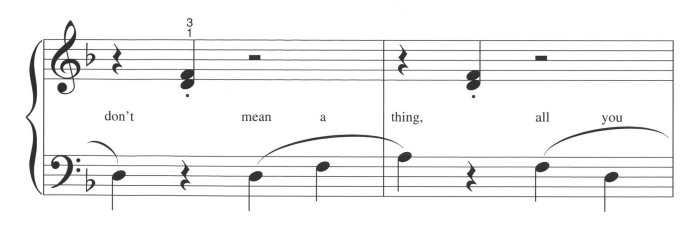

don't   mean   a   thing,   all   you

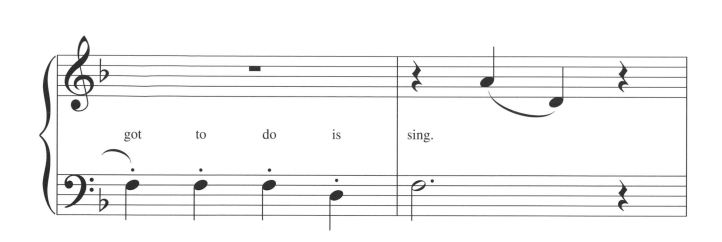

got   to   do   is   sing.

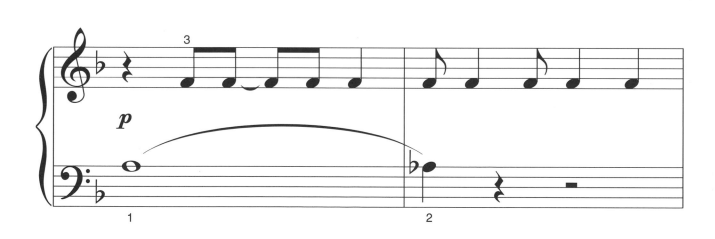

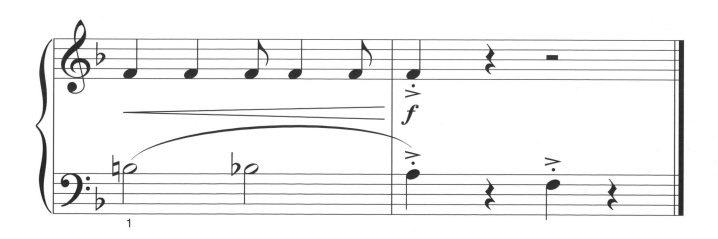

BEYOND THE SEA

Words and Music by CHARLES TRENET,
ALBERT LASRY and JACK LAWRENCE
Arranged by Phillip Keveren

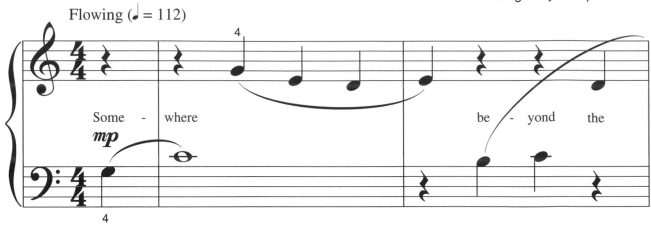

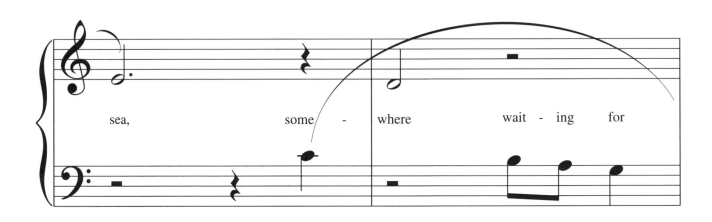

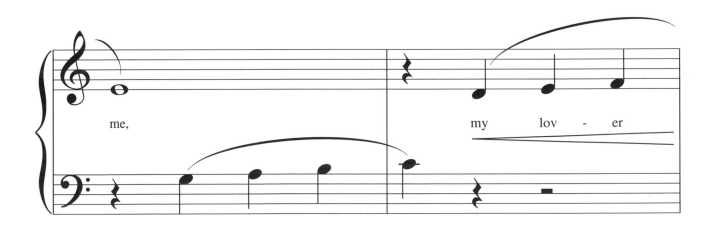

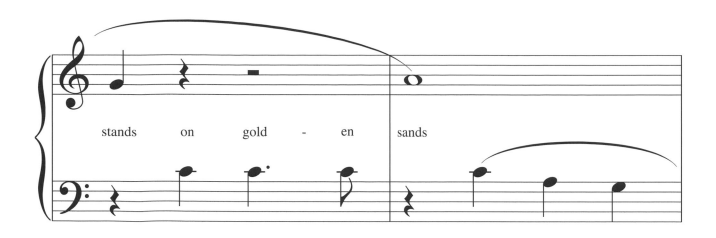

stands on gold - en sands

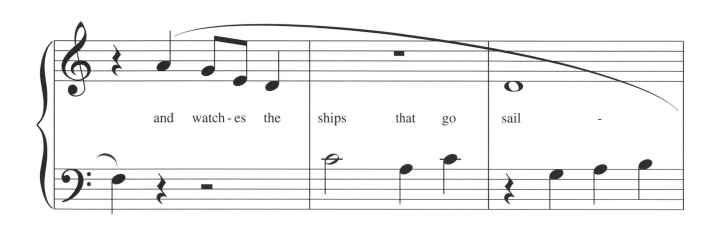

and watch-es the ships that go sail -

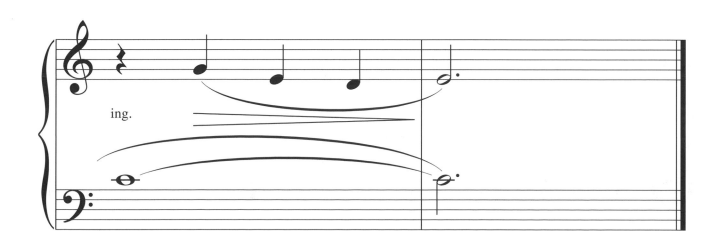

ing.

BYE BYE BLACKBIRD
from PETE KELLY'S BLUES

Lyric by MORT DIXON
Music by RAY HENDERSON
Arranged by Phillip Keveren

Jauntily (♩ = 160)

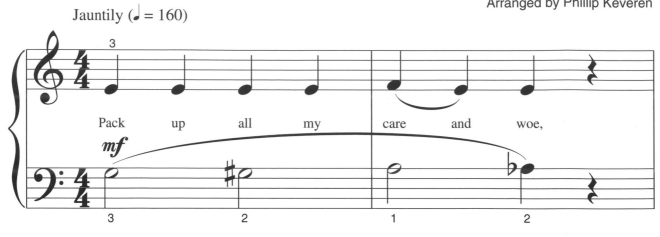

Pack up all my care and woe,

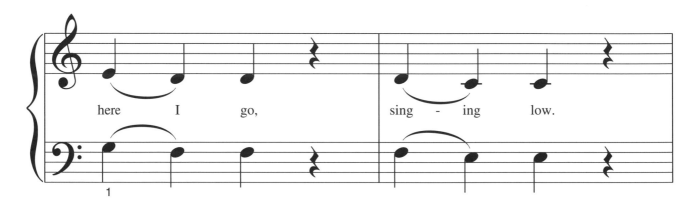

here I go, sing - ing low.

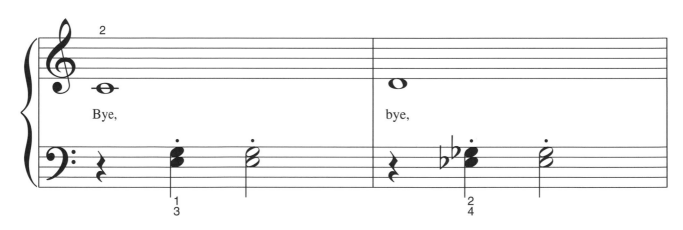

Bye, bye,

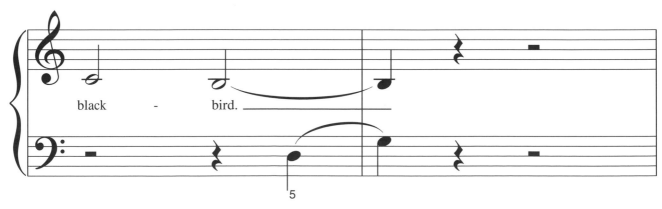

black - bird.

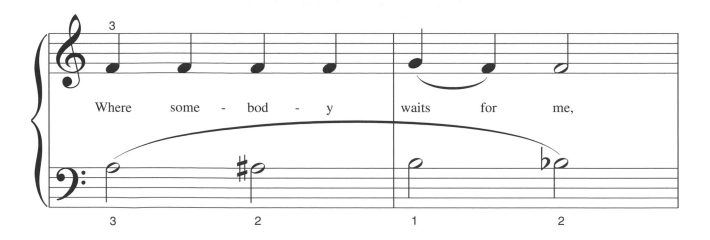

Where some - bod - y waits for me,

sug - ar's sweet, so is she.

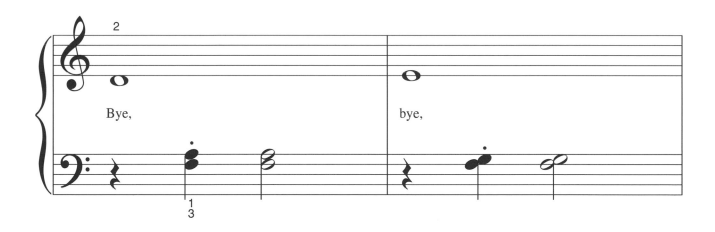

Bye, bye,

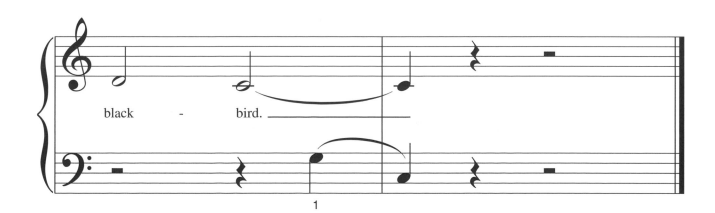

black - bird.

IN THE MOOD

By JOE GARLAND
Arranged by Phillip Keveren

Relaxed Swing (♩ = 126)

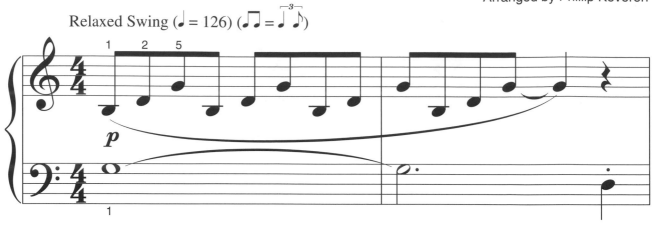

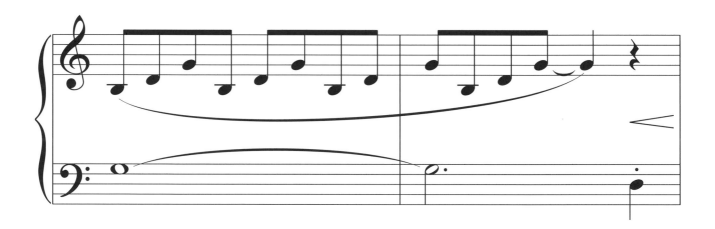

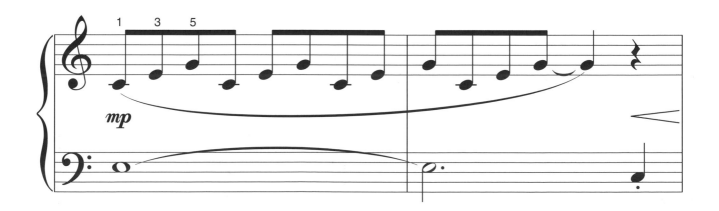

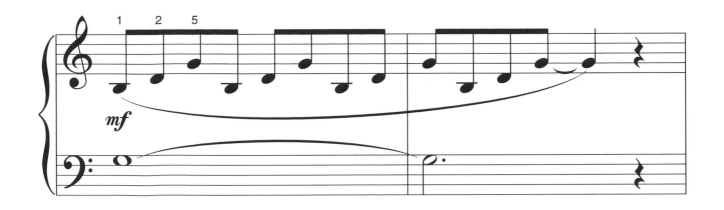

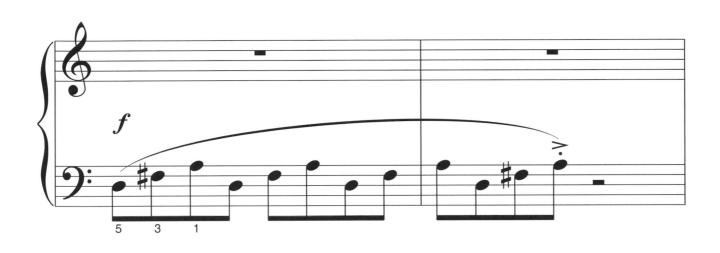

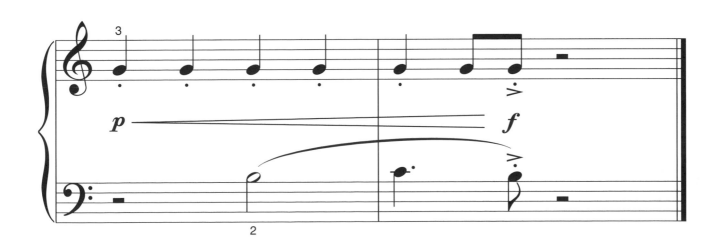

JEANNIE
Theme from I DREAM OF JEANNIE

By HUGH MONTENEGRO
and BUDDY KAYE
Arranged by Phillip Keveren

LINUS AND LUCY

By VINCE GUARALDI
Arranged by Phillip Keveren

Moderately fast (♩ = 144)

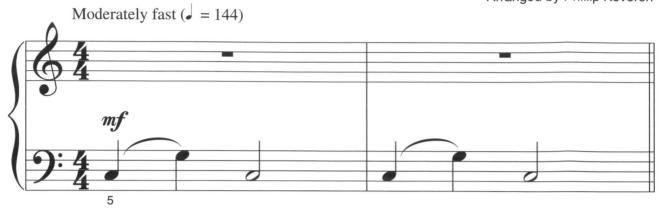

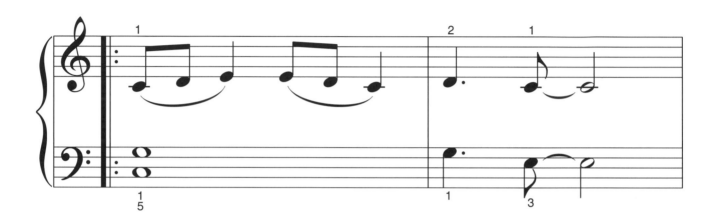

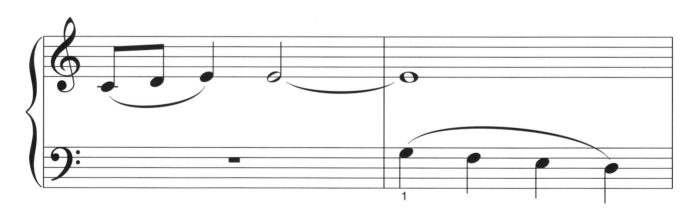

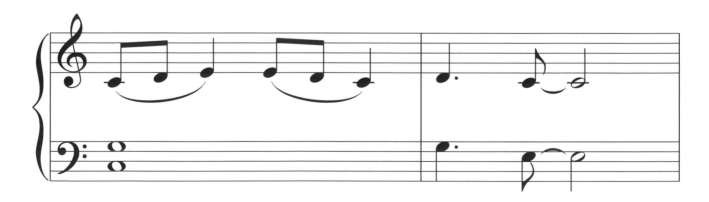

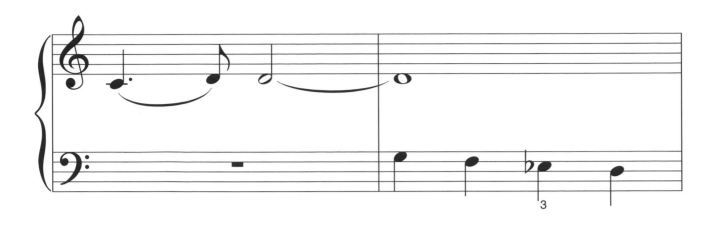

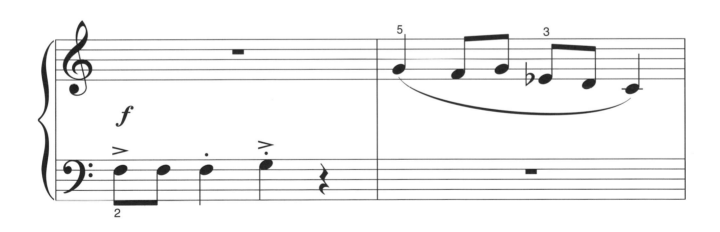

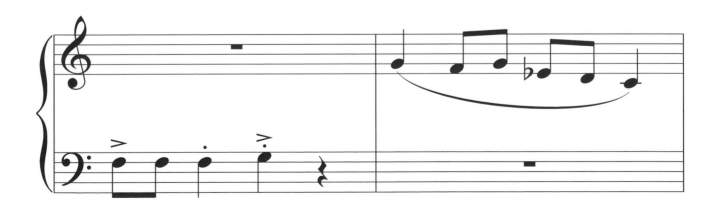

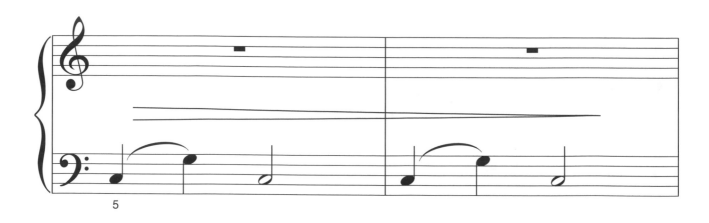

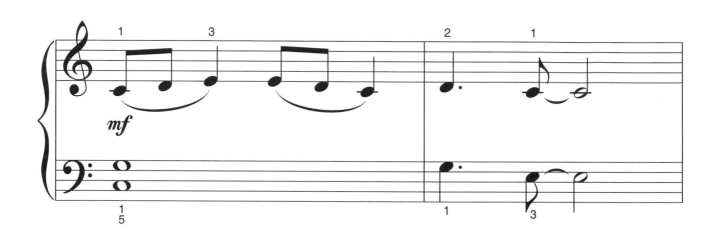

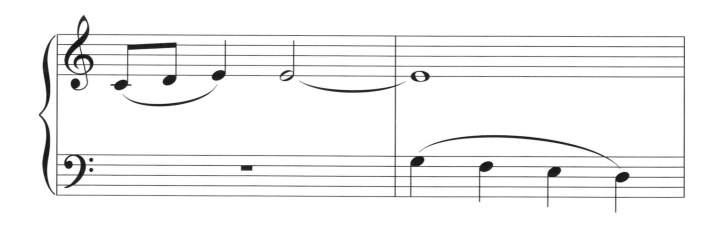

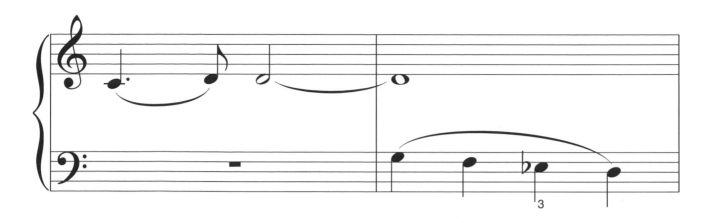

dim. e rit.

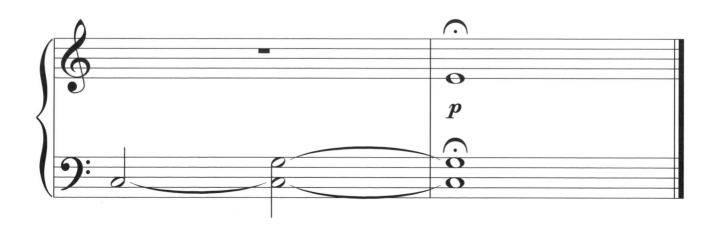

p

MAIRZY DOATS

Words and Music by MILTON DRAKE,
AL HOFFMAN and JERRY LIVINGSTON
Arranged by Phillip Keveren

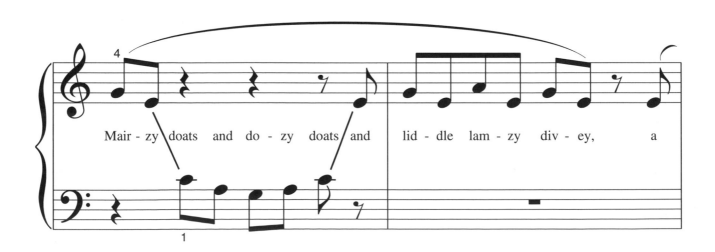

Mair - zy doats and do - zy doats and lid - dle lam - zy div - ey, a

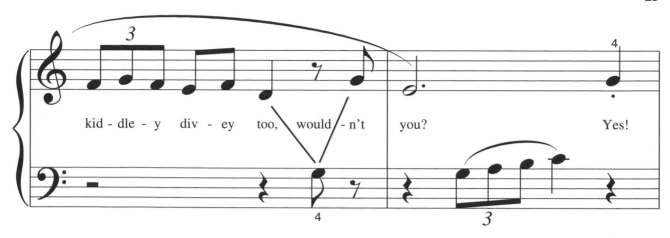

kid - dle - y div - ey too, would-n't you?   Yes!

Mair - zy doats and do - zy doats and lid - dle lam - zy div - ey, a

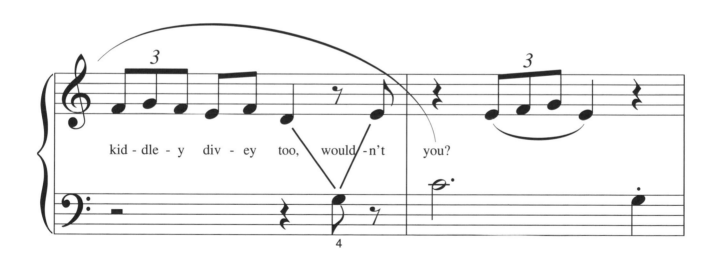

kid - dle - y div - ey too, would -n't you?

NIGHT TRAIN

Words by OSCAR WASHINGTON
and LEWIS C. SIMPKINS
Music by JIMMY FORREST
Arranged by Phillip Keveren

Slow and bluesy ($\quarternote$ = 92)

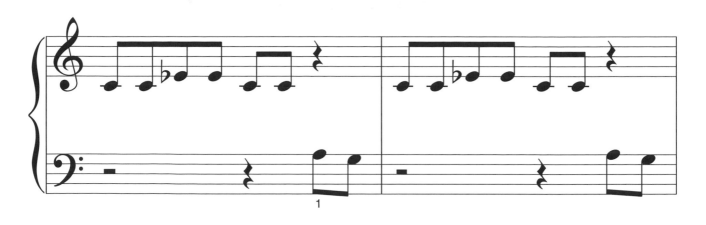

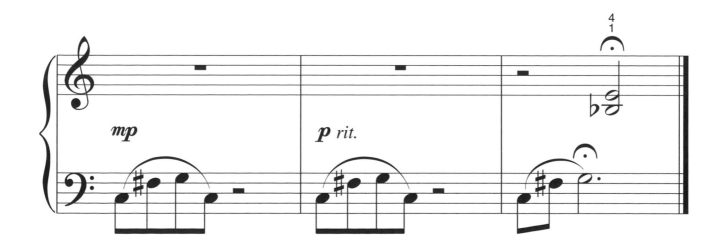

THE ODD COUPLE
Theme from the Paramount Television Series THE ODD COUPLE

By NEAL HEFTI
Arranged by Phillip Keveren

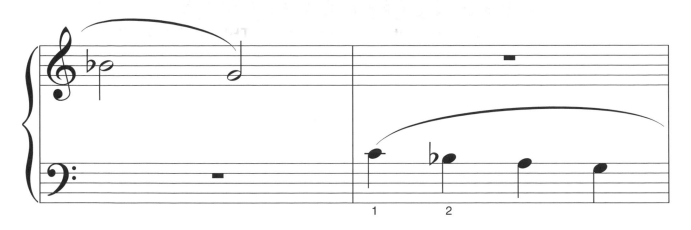

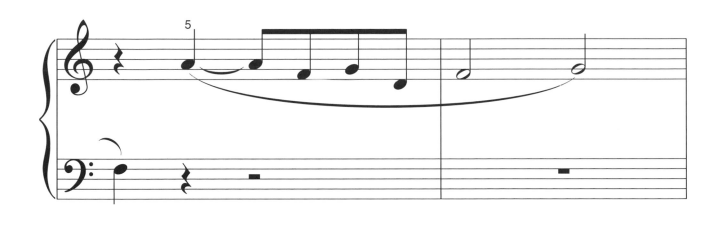

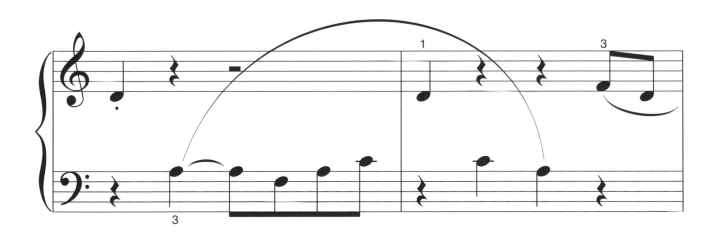

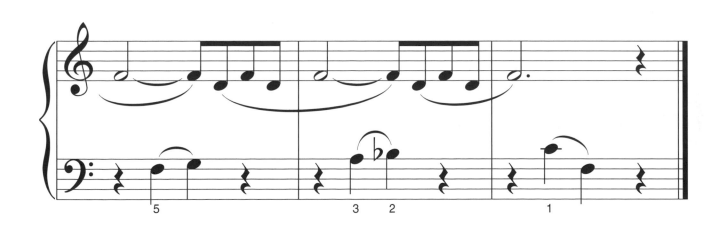

OPUS ONE

Words and Music by
SY OLIVER
Arranged by Phillip Keveren

mel - o - dy's dumb, re - peat an' re - peat, but

if you can swing, it's got a good beat, and

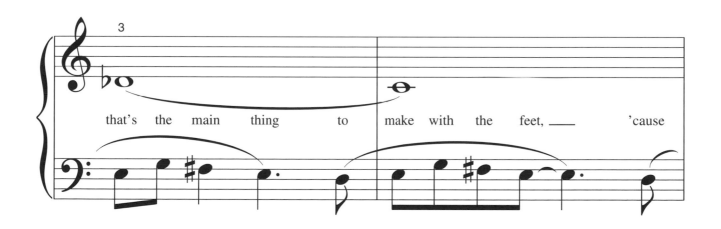

that's the main thing to make with the feet, ___ 'cause

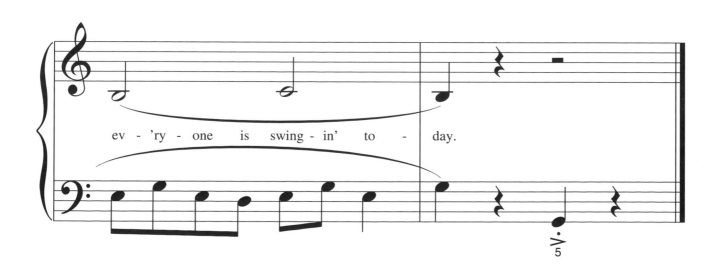

ev - 'ry - one is swing - in' to - day.

SALT PEANUTS

By JOHN "DIZZY" GILLESPIE
and KENNY CLARKE
Arranged by Phillip Keveren

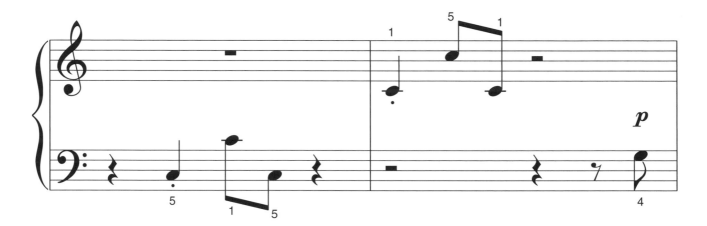

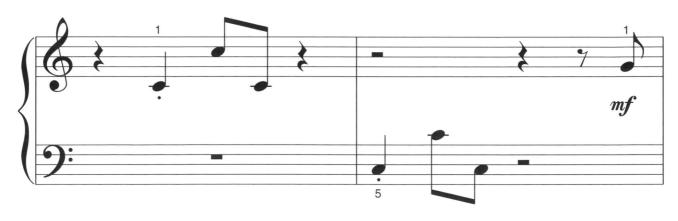

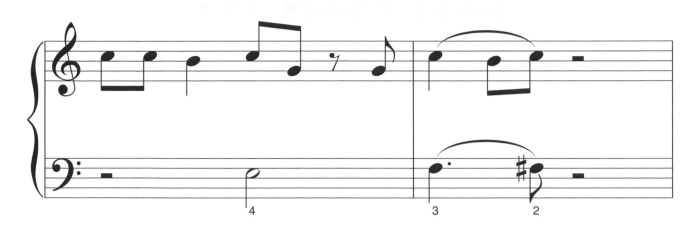

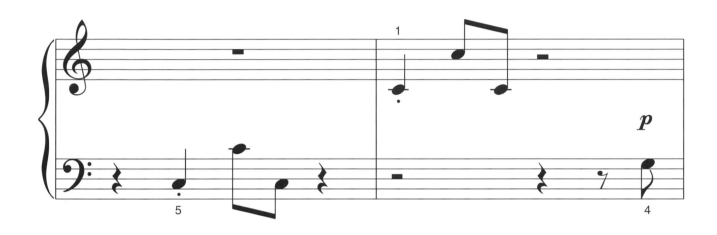

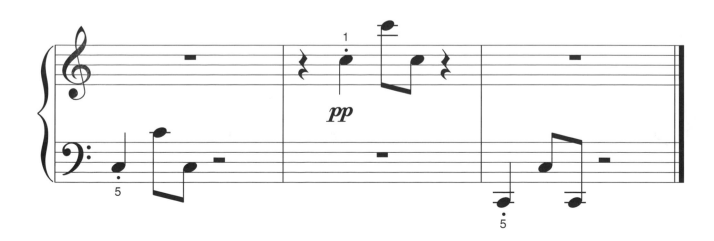

SESAME STREET THEME

Words by BRUCE HART,
JON STONE and JOE RAPOSO
Music by JOE RAPOSO
Arranged by Phillip Keveren

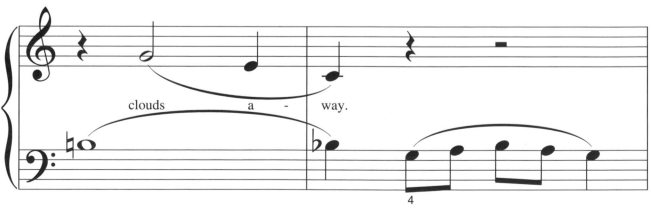

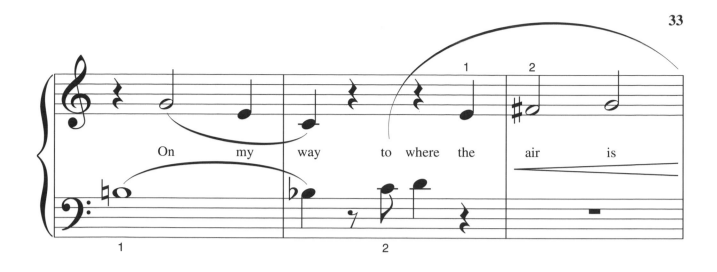

On my way to where the air is

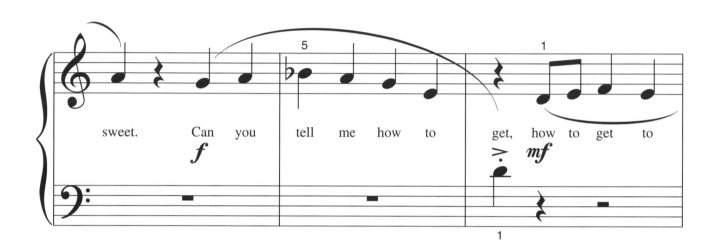

sweet. Can you tell me how to get, how to get to

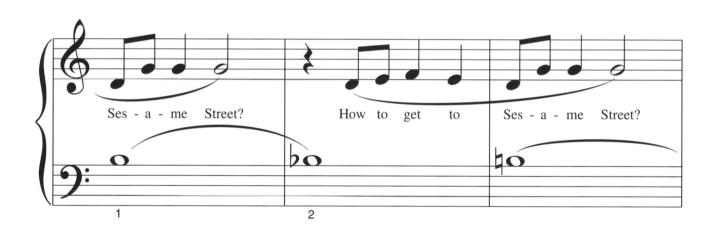

Ses - a - me Street? How to get to Ses - a - me Street?

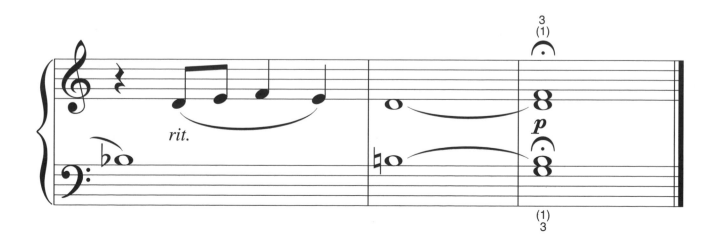

rit.

Sunny

Words and Music by
BOBBY HEBB
Arranged by Phillip Keveren

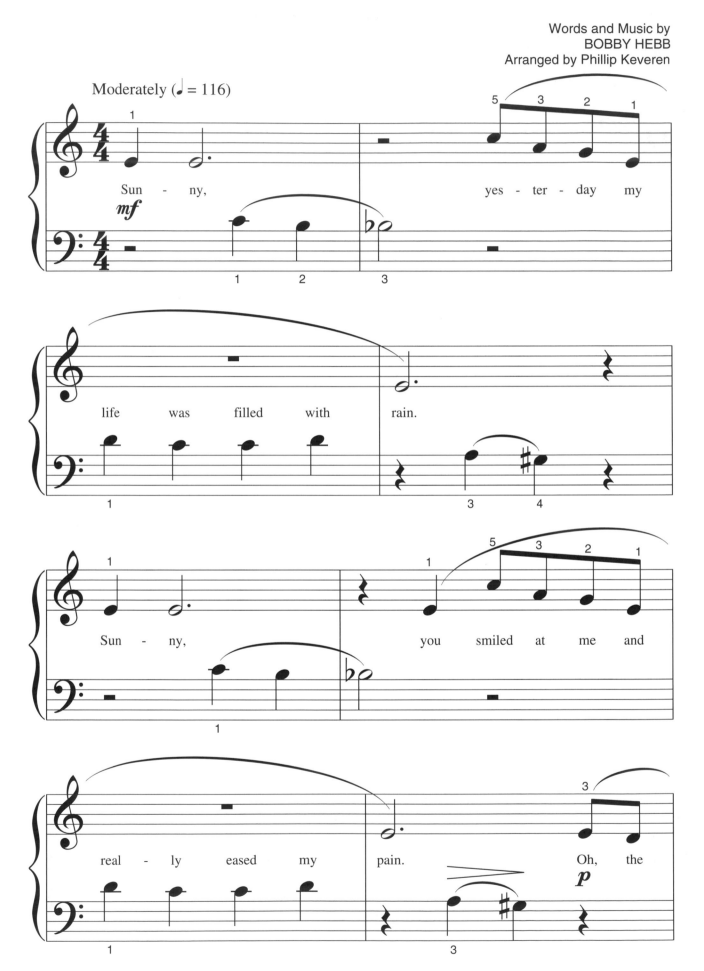

dark days are done, ___ and the bright days are here. ___ My

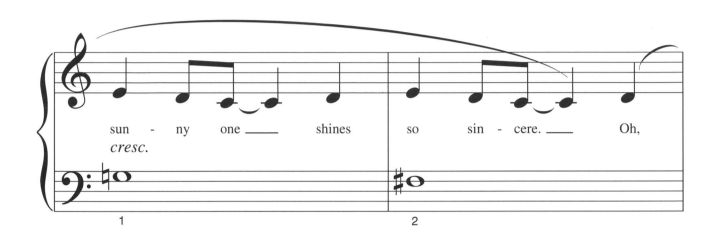

sun - ny one ___ shines so sin - cere. ___ Oh,

cresc.

Sun - ny one so true, I love

f   *p*

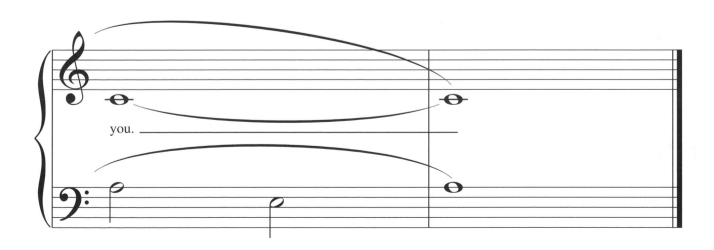

you. ___

THE SURREY WITH THE FRINGE ON TOP

from OKLAHOMA!

Lyrics by OSCAR HAMMERSTEIN II
Music by RICHARD RODGERS
Arranged by Phillip Keveren

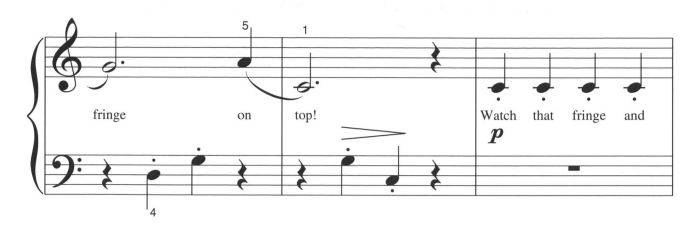

fringe on top! Watch that fringe and

p

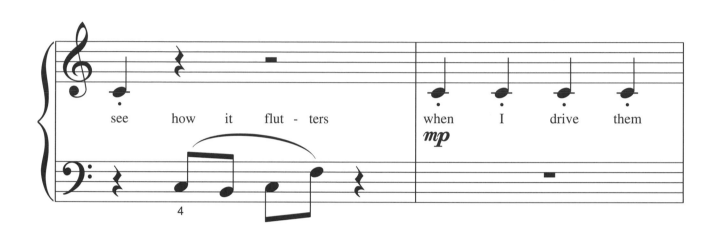

see how it flut - ters when I drive them

mp

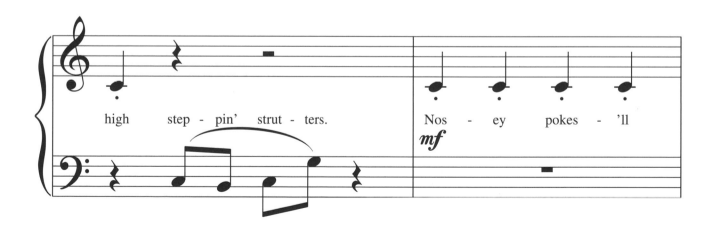

high step - pin' strut - ters. Nos - ey pokes - 'll

mf

peek through their shut-ters and their eyes will pop!

f

TUXEDO JUNCTION

Words by BUDDY FEYNE
Music by ERSKINE HAWKINS,
WILLIAM JOHNSON and JULIAN DASH
Arranged by Phillip Keveren

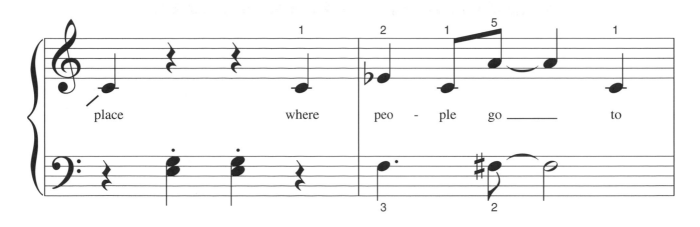

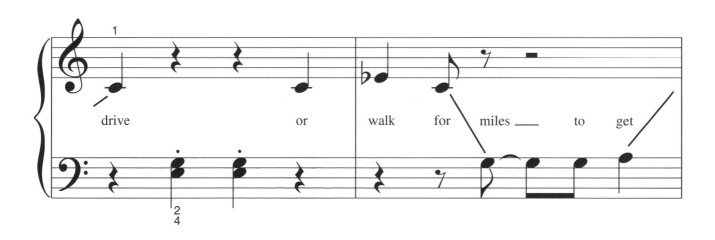

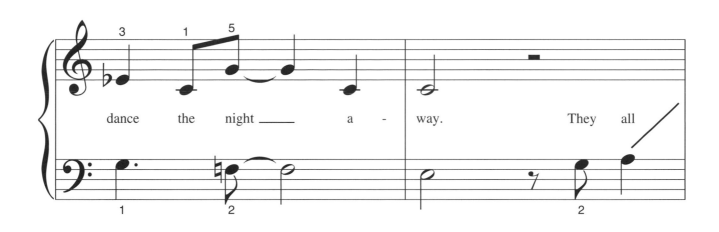

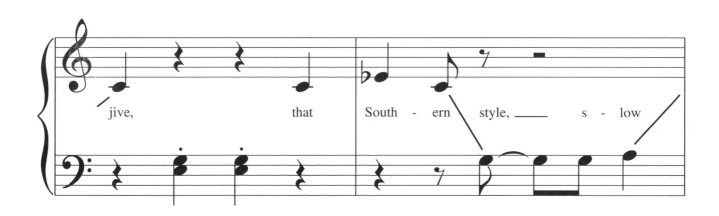

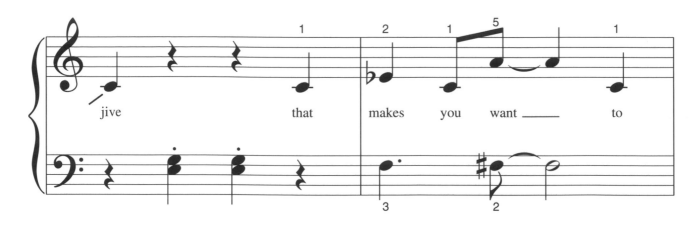

jive   that   makes   you   want _____ to

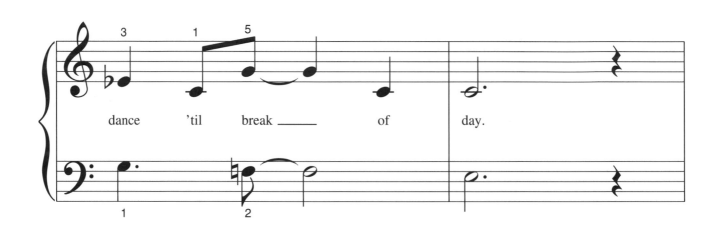

dance   'til   break _____   of   day.

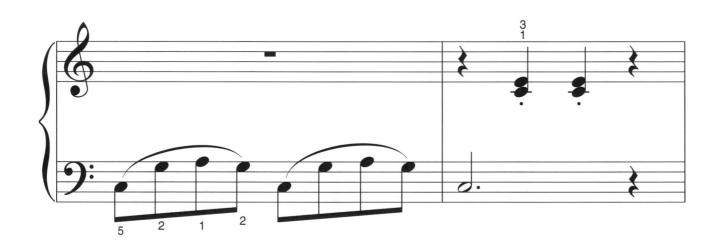

dim. e rit.   *p*